CHILDREN'S AUTHORS

DAVID SHANNON

Tamara L. Britton
ABDO Publishing Company

visit us at
www.abdopublishing.com

Published by ABDO Publishing Company, 8000 West 78th Street, Edina, Minnesota 55439.
Copyright © 2012 by Abdo Consulting Group, Inc. International copyrights reserved in all countries.
No part of this book may be reproduced in any form without written permission from the publisher.
The Checkerboard Library™ is a trademark and logo of ABDO Publishing Company.

Printed in the United States of America, North Mankato, Minnesota.
062011
092011

 PRINTED ON RECYCLED PAPER

Cover Photo: Corbis
Interior Photos: AP Images pp. 13, 20; courtesy David Shannon p. 5; Getty Images pp. 11, 21;
    Photolibrary p. 7; Thinkstock p. 9
*Cover illustration copyright © 1989 by David Shannon from HOW MANY SPOTS DOES A LEOPARD
    HAVE? AND OTHER TALES by Julius Lester. Reprinted by permission of Scholastic Inc. p. 12*
*Reprinted by permission from HOW GEORGIE RADBOURN SAVED BASEBALL by David Shannon.
    Scholastic Inc./The Blue Sky Press. Copyright © 1994 by David Shannon. p. 15*
*Reprinted by permission from NO, DAVID! by David Shannon. Scholastic Inc./The Blue Sky Press.
    Copyright © 1998 by David Shannon. p. 16*
*Reprinted by permission from A BAD CASE OF STRIPES by David Shannon. Scholastic Inc./The Blue
    Sky Press. Copyright © 1998 by David Shannon. p. 19*

Series Coordinator: Megan M. Gunderson; Editors: Megan M. Gunderson, BreAnn Rumsch
Art Direction: Neil Klinepier

Library of Congress Cataloging-in-Publication Data

Britton, Tamara L., 1963-
 David Shannon / Tamara L. Britton.
    p. cm. -- (Children's authors)
 Includes index.
 ISBN 978-1-61783-050-1
 1. Shannon, David, 1959---Juvenile literature. 2. Authors, American--20th century--Biography--
Juvenile literature. 3. Children's stories--Authorship--Juvenile literature. 4. Illustrators--Biography--
Juvenile literature. I. Title.
 PS3569.H3348Z55 2012
 813'.54--dc22
 [B]
                        2011011601

CONTENTS

GO, DAVID!

Have you ever been naughty? Or perhaps you have wanted to be! Naughty or nice, children around the world have found a kindred spirit. They love the rambunctious star of the book *No, David!*

David Shannon is the author and illustrator of *No, David!* The book is about a boy who sometimes does things he shouldn't. It is so popular that Shannon has continued David's story in other books.

Shannon doesn't just write and illustrate his own works. He also illustrates books for other authors. His beautiful pirates are on deck in Jane Yolen's *The Ballad of the Pirate Queens*. And, Shannon has contributed some of the big rigs rolling through Jon Scieszka's Trucktown series.

Shannon didn't plan to become a children's book illustrator. But when the opportunity came to him, he realized it was what he had been preparing for his whole life. With more than 17 million books in print, Shannon's many fans obviously cheer his decision!

Shannon works in a studio above his garage. He calls it "the laboratory"!

YOUNG DAVID

David Shannon was born on October 5, 1959, in Washington, D.C. He is the second of Roger and Martha Shannon's three children. David has an older brother named Mark. His younger sister is named Kimberly.

When David was born, his father was studying medicine at George Washington University. When he completed his training, the family moved to Spokane, Washington. There, Dr. Shannon worked as a **radiologist**.

The Shannon family was very artistic. David's father almost chose a career in medical illustration. And David's grandmother had a degree in fashion illustration.

Growing up, David's family encouraged his interest in art. His father always made sure David had art supplies. He also brought home the paper that protected the X-ray film at his clinic. The thick, orange paper was folded in a way that resembled a book. So, David drew pictures and wrote stories on the paper.

Spokane, Washington

At age five, David created a book about a boy named David. The David in the book is very naughty. The only two words in the story are *no* and *David*. The boy's mother speaks these words because David strains her patience!

In addition to drawing, David also liked to read. As he read, the pictures that illustrated the stories inspired him. So, David began to draw pirates, knights, and baseball players, too.

School Days

At school, David's teachers encouraged him to draw. He often participated in class projects that included drawing. By the time he was a high school student, David knew he wanted to be an artist.

David decided to attend art school after he graduated from high school. He liked to draw, but he wanted to be sure his work would provide financial security. And, he was not sure what **genre** appealed to him most. At college, David could explore different art forms and discover which he found most interesting.

When he was 19 years old, David moved from Spokane to Los Angeles, California. There, he attended the Art Center College of Design in nearby Pasadena.

The course work at the Art Center was challenging. David struggled to get all the work done. He often stayed awake all night long working on paintings! But as he worked, he came to realize the type of artist he wanted to be. He wanted to become an illustrator.

Pasadena, California

PROFESSIONAL ILLUSTRATOR

Shannon graduated from the Art Center in 1983 with a bachelor of fine arts degree. In college, he had learned to illustrate political articles. He hoped to find work illustrating **editorials** for newspapers and magazines. So, Shannon moved to New York City, New York, to earn his living as an illustrator.

It was not easy to find work in New York City. Shannon visited many publications and showed editors his **portfolio**. Yet jobs were few, and money was scarce.

Still, Shannon **persevered**. At home, he continued to practice his art. As his illustrations improved, he got more work assignments. In time, his editorial illustrations appeared in the *New York Times* and magazines such as *Time* and *Rolling Stone*.

Soon, Shannon had work as a regular contributor to several respected publications. One of these was the *New York Times Book Review*. One day, one of

Jean Feiwel (left) with Ann M. Martin, author of the popular Baby-Sitters Club series

Shannon's drawings appeared next to a review of a children's book. The drawing caught the eye of editor Jean Feiwel. She worked for Scholastic, a children's book publishing company.

Feiwel was looking for an artist to illustrate a picture book by author Julius Lester. The book was called *How Many Spots Does a Leopard Have? And Other Tales*. Feiwel contacted Shannon and asked him if he wanted the job. Shannon thought the project sounded interesting. So, he said yes. It was a decision that would change the course of his career.

A New Direction

How Many Spots Does a Leopard Have? was published in
1989. The collection of folktales was named an American Library
Association (ALA) Notable Children's Book.
The book did so well that other editors
began to send stories to Shannon. They
wanted him to illustrate their books, too.

Shannon had not considered being
a children's book illustrator. He thought
illustrating the Lester book would be
a one-time project. He also thought
children's book illustrators had to draw
cute fuzzy animals, like bunnies. He
didn't want to be stuck doing that!

Still, Shannon decided to continue
working on children's books. He illustrated *The Rough-Face Girl*
and *The Boy Who Lived with the Seals*. Both books were Native
American folktales by author Rafe Martin.

Shannon also illustrated two books by best-selling author Jane Yolen. *Encounter* is a story about Christopher Columbus and his first contact with the native Taino people of San Salvador Island in the Bahamas. In *The Ballad of the Pirate Queens*, two female pirates defend their ship from attack.

Shannon soon saw that illustrations in children's books were very **diverse**. They weren't all of cute little

American artist N.C. Wyeth's images were a big influence on Shannon's style.

animals! Children's books were full of pirates, knights, and baseball players. Shannon realized he could make a living as an adult drawing what he had loved to draw as a child.

AUTHOR AND ILLUSTRATOR

Shannon continued to find work as a children's book illustrator. He illustrated two more books of folktales, this time written by his brother Mark. *Gawain and the Green Knight* is a **medieval** tale of Gawain, one of King Arthur's knights. *The Acrobat and the Angel* is another medieval tale. It is the story of a French boy who survives the **bubonic plague**.

Readers enjoyed Shannon's illustrations. Many asked why he did not write a book of his own. Shannon did indeed have some story ideas. So in 1994, he produced the first book that he both illustrated and wrote.

How Georgie Radbourn Saved Baseball is the story of an imaginary time in America when baseball is illegal. Without baseball, the seasons are stuck on winter. Springtime never comes! The *New York Times Book Review* named *Georgie Radbourn* the Best Illustrated Children's Book.

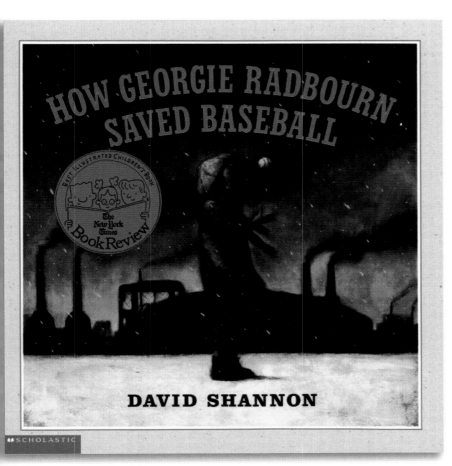

In college, Shannon had learned to illustrate **editorial** pieces about serious ideas. He used dark colors to illustrate these ideas. At the same time, he also liked to draw cold, gray days.

In *Georgie Radbourn*, Shannon's illustrations of the long winter are dark and cloudy. Reviewers commented that his use of dark colors is well-suited to his story. They create a dramatic mood.

BACK TO THE FUTURE

But *How Georgie Radbourn Saved Baseball* was not really Shannon's first book. Shannon's mother had his first book. She had been saving it for many years. In 1998, she sent Shannon the book he had written when he was five. The book was on the faded orange paper that had once protected X-ray film. It would lead to one of Shannon's best-known works.

Shannon examined the book

closely. Its eight stapled-together pages were full of a young child's drawings. The stick-figure character named David had a large, round head and pointy teeth.

In the story, David's behavior is bad! He jumps up and down on the bed. He tries to get cookies without permission. Eventually, David is punished. But he still knows he is loved.

Shannon decided to re-create the book. At first, he drew David in his normal art style. So, David looked like a regular boy. But the story did not work. Shannon realized that David really was a stick figure with a large, round head and pointy teeth. When Shannon drew David as he had done when he was five, the character and the story came alive.

Shannon's editor at Scholastic, Bonnie Verburg, was not sure the unusual book would appeal to children. But when she saw it, she decided to take a chance. This turned out to be the right decision. *No, David!* became a 1999 **Caldecott Honor Book**.

No, David! *won several honors. It was named an ALA Notable Children's Book and the* **New York Times** *Best Illustrated Book of the Year.*

EVOLVING

Shannon continued to illustrate books by other authors. He created bold, action-filled illustrations for Jon Scieszka's *Robot Zot*. But after the success of *No, David!*, Shannon also kept writing his own books.

When creating a book, Shannon first writes the story. Then, he reads over it several times. When he has an idea of who the story's characters are, he starts drawing them.

Shannon sketches each illustration several times in little pictures called thumbnails. In time, the story he sees in his imagination begins to emerge on the page. Then, Shannon creates full-sized drawings. This is his favorite part!

When the drawings are complete, Shannon puts the words and pictures together. This makes a model that shows what the final book will look like. When he is satisfied, Shannon paints the art using acrylic paints and colored pencils.

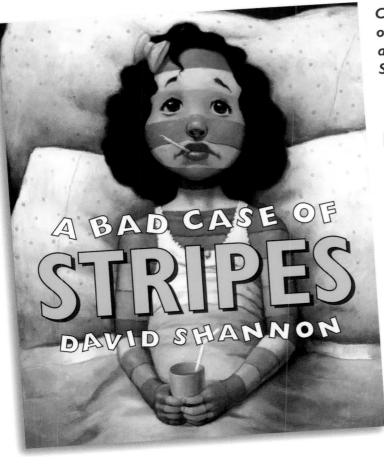

Color helps set the tone of a work of art. Bright colors are happy, and dark colors are less so. Today, Shannon creates very happy art!

In this way, Shannon has created many great books. *The Amazing Christmas Extravaganza* is the story of out-of-control Christmas decorating. In *A Bad Case of Stripes*, a little girl is sick in bed with stripes! And in *Duck on a Bike*, barnyard animals zoom around on two wheels.

As he has **evolved** as an artist, Shannon's work has become more colorful and playful. While his earlier art is rich with dark colors, Shannon's more recent work uses brighter colors. *The Amazing Christmas Extravaganza* and *A Bad Case of Stripes* are full of dazzling color!

ARTIST TODAY

Shannon married in 1988. His wife, Heidi, is a voice actress. She has voiced characters on the television series *Rugrats* and in Star Wars video games. The Shannons have

a daughter named Emma. The family lives in Burbank, California, with their West Highland white terrier, Fergus.

Shannon still keeps the faded orange book he wrote when he was five. It has inspired much success. Besides *No, David!*, Shannon has written and illustrated three additional David books. They are *David Goes to School*, *David Gets in Trouble*, and *It's Christmas, David!* He is

The Shannon family's dog, Fergus, appears in every book Shannon illustrates.

also exploring a younger version of David with the Diaper David book series.

Shannon works at home in a studio above his garage. He keeps a notebook in which he writes down ideas for new projects. Fans of Shannon's books hope his notebook's list of ideas is a very long one!

Shannon (right) with fellow children's authors Henry Winkler (left) and Barney Saltzberg (center)

GLOSSARY

bubonic plague (byoo-BAH-nihk PLAYG) - a disease marked by chills, fever, weakness, and swollen glands called buboes. It spreads to humans through the bites of fleas carrying the disease.

Caldecott Honor Book - a runner-up for the Caldecott Medal. The Caldecott Medal is an award the American Library Association gives to the artist who illustrated the year's best picture book.

diverse - made up of unlike pieces or qualities.

editorial - a newspaper or magazine article intended to give an opinion about a certain topic.

evolve - to develop gradually.

genre (ZHAHN-ruh) - a type of art, music, or literature.

medieval - of or belonging to the Middle Ages. The Middle Ages was a period in European history from about AD 500 to 1500.

persevere - to keep doing something even though it is difficult.

portfolio - a selection of a person's work.

radiologist - a doctor who uses X-rays to find out what diseases people have and treat them.

WEB SITES

To learn more about David Shannon, visit ABDO Publishing Company online. Web sites about David Shannon are featured on our Book Links page. These links are routinely monitored and updated to provide the most current information available.
www.abdopublishing.com

INDEX